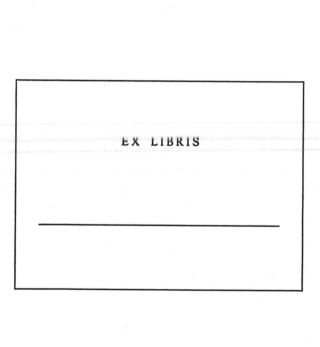

EX LIBRIS

What

Do We

Mean When

We Say God?

Compiled by

Deidre Sullivan

CADER BOOKS

DOUBLEDAY
New York   London   Toronto   Sydney   Auckland

What
Do We
Mean When
We Say
God?

PUBLISHED BY DOUBLEDAY

a division of Bantam Doubleday Dell Publishing Group, Inc.

666 Fifth Avenue, New York, New York 10103

DOUBLEDAY
and the portrayal of an anchor with a dolphin
are trademarks of Doubleday, a division of
Bantam Doubleday Dell Publishing Group, Inc.

Library of Congress Cataloging-in-Publication Data

What do we mean when we say God? / compiled by Deidre Sullivan.
— 1st ed.
p.   cm.
"Cader books."
1. God—Quotations, maxims, etc.   2. God—Public opinion.
3. Public opinion—United States.   I. Sullivan, Deidre A.
BL205.W46   1991
211—dc20   90-32031
                                                                CIP

ISBN 0-385-41132-4

February 1991

1   3   5   7   9   10   8   6   4   2

First Edition

Acknowledgments

Many people have given graciously and generously of their time and thoughts in helping to provide this book with its richness and diversity. The authors extend their thanks to Catherine Browning, Michael Carlisle, Rick Cimino, Frank Don, Ron and Patsy Fraser, Dorothy Flanagan, C.N.D., Seth Godin, Karina Haywood, R.S.M., Victoria Hobbs, Heather Evans, Pam Keld, Annabelle Krigstein, Joan Magnetti, R.S.C.J., Cora McLaughlin, R.S.C.J., Moira McLaughlin, R.S.C., Geraldine McInerney, Tom Phillips, Walter Raquet, Dominica Rocchio, S.C., Vicki Rose, Marian Salzman, Ira Schreck, Renee Schwartz, Rosemary Sheehan, R.S.C.J., Lottchen Shivers, Joanna Stingray, Gregory Stock, Dee Dee Isaacs Sturr, Dennis Stovall and his seventh and eighth grade English classes at Clark Junior High School in Anchorage, David Sultanik, Shirley Thormann, Ellen Watson, and Steve Haweeli, Victoria Willis, Maura Wogan, the Archdiocese of New York, Convent of the Sacred Heart in Greenwich, Connecticut, the Christian Appalachian Project in Martin, Kentucky, the Stuart Country Day School in Princeton, New Jersey, the Wesleyan Holiness Chapel and Academy in Mt. Pleasant, Michigan.

Special thanks are owed to Jeffrey Zaslow and all of his loyal readers who shared their thoughts with us.

We are also appreciative of the support and dedication of the Doubleday staff in all phases of completing this book. Our editor, Paul Bresnick, has made no secret of his overwhelming enthusiasm from the moment this book was first suggested, and has been essential in rallying the troops throughout the publishing process. We also thank Mark Garofalo, Jim Bell, and Whitney Cookman for their valuable contributions. Furthermore, we would like to thank Nancy Evans and the many editors at Bantam Doubleday Dell who gladly aided in eliciting responses for the book.

Finally, we extend our special thanks to Keith Haring for his inspiration and support.

Introduction

This book takes one of the simplest and most essential questions—What Do We Mean When We Say God?—and turns it into a window on the spirit and soul of contemporary America. It started as a friendly conversation between myself and Michael Cader of Cader Books, which we then turned into a conversation with thousands of people all across America.

For some time now there has been a strong feeling that God is very much in the air: from Alcoholics Anonymous and other recovery groups to the rise and fall of Islamic fundamentalism, from the evangelical Christianity movement and the evolution of modern Israel to the increasing religious scrutiny of contemporary movies, books, and television, the name of God is invoked in all sorts of new ways, and all too often the search for what all these different people really mean when they speak of God is left unpursued.

That is the course we set on, to talk to as many different people from as many different faiths all over the country to find out just what God means to them. We spoke to people of all ages and all occupations, members of established clergy and leaders of some of the most radical religious movements, believers and nonbelievers, schoolchildren and the elderly—thousands of people in all. The responses we garnered were necessarily reflective of the diverse kinds of people we interviewed.

We were then faced with the very tough decisions of who to include in the book. Everyone we interviewed spoke to us in a genuine, thoughtful, and highly personal way, and we are grateful to them all for making this book possible. But from this, we wanted to fashion a collection that would be simultaneously thoughtful, touching, inspiring, challenging, even at times disturbing, while remaining faithful and respectful to everyone's firmly held beliefs.

For many people, the whole notion of this book was preposterous—God has told us Himself and the answer is in the Bible, we were often told. Others said that talking about God was inappropriate, that God shouldn't be named. And others still felt equally sure of the scriptures of different faiths, or of revelations of a much more personal kind.

And so in selecting the entries you will find in this book, we tried to remain faithful to our original objectives: to present the widest possible array of different ways of thinking about God—and feeling and seeing and finding and worshiping God—as possible. The book includes comments from Christian fundamentalists and orthodox Jews, New Age mystics and trance channels, mediators and militants—and much more beyond that. Along with our wish for diversity, we tried to reflect the balance of religious affiliations in the country today. So you will certainly find more entries from Christians than from any other faith, more Jews than Muslims, more Muslims than siddha yoga practitioners. This does not mean that the Christian entries were better, or that they "won" in terms of the quality of their expression. They are simply meant to reflect the balance of the overall sampling.

At many times we have also intentionally juxtaposed provocative comments from radically different perspectives. Our point in doing this is not to judge or take sides, but to challenge, to provoke thought, and to offer a constant reminder that for every deeply held vision of faith there is often another, equally sincere, equally sacred belief. One person's blasphemy is often another person's truth.

In showcasing the beliefs of so many other people, it's only fair to give you a sense of my own beliefs. When I first started working on *What Do We Mean When We Say God?* I saw the project as simply a good idea and that was it. I had always been interested in the role that religion played in American culture but I had had no personal interest in the topic of God. When I started the book, I was agnostic. I had a vague idea of God "out there" but never gave the topic much serious thought. Although I'd grown up in a Catholic family and attended the Convent of the Sacred Heart, religion was never pushed on me in either environment. God was presented as a choice, but it was a choice I never wanted to make. Religious belief was something that was fine for the nuns but not for me. Over the course of the year, as I've worked on this book, that has changed.

Working on this project and talking to so many different people was—at times—a very moving experience. As each person I interviewed revealed something about themselves, they also taught me something about myself. This was a wonderful gift.

These conversations awakened my own awareness of God. A year ago, an awakening of this sort is the last thing I would have predicted.

Am I a born-again Christian? In the fundamentalist sense of the word, no. I don't have a day marked in my diary when I was "saved." But in the larger, cosmic, mystical sense: yes. My change in belief didn't happen overnight. Rather, it's been a continual process of rebirth, one which I hope will continue for the rest of my life.

Whether you use this book to explore new ways of believing or to confirm your existing beliefs, I hope the investigation is as productive and as influential for you as it was for me.

I laugh when I think that the question I asked everyone else was the one that I most needed to ask myself.

—Deidre Sullivan

What
Do We
Mean When
We Say God?

"WHERE CAN you find God? On the pages of the Scriptures—especially in the New Testament in the four Gospels."

Donald J. Anderson, Age 65, Pastor,
Faith Community Fellowship, Jackson, Mississippi

"THE QUESTION to ask is 'What is truth?' I feel men can discover truth, but they don't create it. God is truth. He created all truth. Truth to me is: things as they are, as they were, and as they will be."

Anne Williams, Age 37, Telephone Operator,
Alpine, Utah

"GOD CREATED US in His image. Since then, human beings have been trying to create God in their image. The word 'god' comes from the Anglo-Saxon. It means 'one who is greeted.' God is the mystery of life we greet. Experiencing God is like saying 'Hey!' Sometimes we experience the mystery of God in a flower, in another person, in ourselves. The mystery expresses itself in everything. When we recognize it and try to put a word on it, it's 'Hey.' "

Daniel Martin, Age 42, Catholic Priest,
Rye, New York

We are born believing. A man bears beliefs, as a tree bears apples.

Ralph Waldo Emerson

"GOD IS WITH me almost every thinking moment of the day. There are times when I don't think about it, but He's there. Any time I have to make major decisions, I say to myself, '. . . with the help of God.' As an orthodox Jew, we have prayers for most of our daily activities. For instance when I wake up in the morning, He's in my presence immediately. I say a prayer after I go to the bathroom, after I wash my hands, and before I eat something. These are blessings. I understand that God controls me even to the extent of all my body functions and everyday activities. I pray that He guides me and that He controls my way and my way will be correct. The expression that we have is 'God willing.' Everything that happens is God willing the way it is supposed to be. In other words, there is destiny in everything. There's also another Hebrew expression that means 'Also this is only for the good'—even if what's happening may seem seriously bad at the moment."

Miriam Gold, Age 39, Housewife,
Brooklyn, New York

"WHEN I WAS a child, God meant an old guy with a long white beard. When I grew intelligent, He meant nothing. Now as I grow old, God means perfect love."

Mary Jane Monroe, Age 64, Housewife,
San Antonio, Texas

"A MAN without God is like a teenager with a powerful car."

Mary Jo Cooper, Age 77, Unity Minister,
Laguna Hills, California

Jesus said to him, "I am the way, and the truth, and the life; no one comes to the Father, but through me."

John 14:6

"PHYSICS doesn't leave any room for magic—there can't be an omnipotent being pulling our strings and determining our future. Any activity that is designed to appease (or beg favors from) this mythical being is probably not productive. Instead of using religion as an excuse for not going to a friend's wedding, declaring a war, or persecuting someone, let's concentrate on what God really is: doing something nice for another person with no hope of being repaid. Taking care of nature. Being nice for no good reason. Never rationalizing behavior that hurts another. Always giving more than you get. That's my God."

Seth Godin, Age 30, Video Producer,
Mt. Vernon, New York

"My opinion of God is that everyone sees God in their own way. I see God as being black because I'm black. In the same breath, a white person might see God as being white. I have no objection because we both have the same God, we just see Him differently."

Vernon Hodge, Age 15,
Bronx, New York

A conviction, akin to religious feeling, of the rationality or intangibility of the world lies behind all scientific work of a higher order. This firm belief, a belief bound up with deep feeling, in a superior mind that reveals itself in the world of experience, represents my conception of God.

Albert Einstein

"THE BIBLE is a blueprint for living. And my image of God is a biblical image. God is personal and triune, not a cosmic force as in Eastern thought. He's different from us, but we are—of course—created in His image and the only way to be accepted by Him is through His son Jesus Christ. That's the essence of Christianity, and a lot of the craziness that's going on in the evangelical world would be done away with if we just stuck to those basic concepts."

Gary DeMar, Age 40, President, American Vision,
Atlanta, Georgia

I do not pretend to know where many ignorant men are sure—that is all agnosticism means.

Clarence Darrow

"**I** BELIEVE that you can call God by any name because we firmly believe that there is no name which is not God's name. All sounds have been created by God. So any sound which is created should name Him, should address Him, should be His name. The rustling of the leaves, the sound of the ocean and singing of the birds, all glorify God.

God has given us freedom to do our own thinking and to ask our own questions. He in effect says listen to all that I have said, but make your own decision. He encourages us to ask questions. That's why there are so many branches of Hinduism. We are allowed to choose our own path and there is so much we can choose from. I look at the whole world of scripture, not just Hindu or Muslim or Christian ones. I believe God is in everything. There are many instances of where God has spoken."

Gopeenath Galagali, Age 29, Hindu Preacher,
Nashville, Tennessee

"GOD IS caring like a mother and strong and strict like a father. So God is both mother and father."

Jason Hernandez, Age 17,
Bronx, New York

"I FEEL such wonder when I think about the human spirit and its attempts to search for the ultimate. That very stretching out seems to me to be an art. God reaching out to humans, and humans reaching out to God—it's a love affair, and it's not all one way. I love the romance between humans and God. To me, art is the expression of that romance. The word 'God' is a useful tool, but it doesn't have much meaning because it points to something that can't be known, but only experienced. It begins and ends any conversation about itself."

Betty Sue Flowers, Age 43, English Professor,
University of Texas, Austin

"A FRIEND told me this story once. Imagine that there is a grasshopper sitting on a milkweed plant near the railroad tracks in Montana. And the Great Northern Railroad goes by, the Empire Builder, and it creates a huge ruckus and the milkweed starts to bounce and bob and weave and the grasshopper looks around. Does he know why it's happening? He doesn't. And that is sort of the way I feel about God. There is obviously something happening but it is beyond my understanding."

Howard Weaver, Age 39, Editor-in-Chief,
Anchorage *Daily News*,
Anchorage, Alaska

Faith is to believe what we do not see, and the reward of this faith is to see what we believe.

Augustine

"THERE'S a polluted aspect to the word 'God.' In our culture, we're surrounded by either a self-centered secularism or just crazy religion. You've either got the secular humanists who think God talk is garbage and that it's silly to raise the issue. Or you get the crazy people who think they've got God in their hip pocket and that God is going to do people in. So there are a lot of reasons why the word 'God' has a brutalizing effect on people. And here I try and talk about God as that boundless mystery and words like 'lover' and 'friend' and 'mercy' come to mind. Most people don't want to believe in God at all. They don't want faith. They want certainty."

Alan Jones, Age 50, Dean, Grace Cathedral,
San Francisco, California

I believe in the incomprehensibility of God.

Honoré de Balzac

"MY GOAL in life is to worship Allah. That is my reason for being. Muslims believe that God is actively involved in the world; therefore, Muslims should be actively involved in the world as a reflection of that worship. Everything I do has to connote worship: my marriage, my conduct, my work—even talking on the phone is part of worship. Islam really expands the notion of worship. It's not just ritual or prayer—although rituals are important (praying five times a day, fasting, etc. . . .). But every act you do should connote worship because you should always be in remembrance of Allah. I think this simplicity and wholism is what attracts people to Islam."

Amer Haleem, Age 32, Editor, *Islamic Horizons,*
Oak Lawn, Illinois

"MY CHURCH is the church of the eternally fascinated. Because the way it looks to me is that God is infinite. Religions don't hold up under the light of scrutiny so I try to be like the swan who separates milk from water. I just chuck the rest. It *is* all really one. You take a glass of water, that water has passed through Abraham Lincoln's body, Hitler's body, a gazelle in Africa's body. We're all one. Past, present, and future exist simultaneously; if I didn't blow my nose this morning, then Jesus couldn't have been crucified. It's all inextricably bound."

Anthony Adams, Age 37, Screenwriter,
Sherman Oaks, California

"WHEN I WAS in high school, people talked about the Gospel and about how God sent His son Jesus to earth. I thought that's nice, but I'm doing fine on my own thank-you-very-much. I thought God was for B students, and I always got A's. I kept this prideful attitude right through Harvard, Harvard Business School. During business school, my father contracted brain cancer and died. A few months later, my mother died of alcoholism. Even though I had a great job on Wall Street, I didn't have a lot of joy in my life. I began to pray and I didn't expect anybody to listen, but God did. I then went to a Bible study with a friend and for the first time in my life, the Gospel message hit home. It affected me profoundly. It makes so much sense. I decided to ask Jesus to be my personal savior. I can honestly say my life has never been so good. I feel blessed. Having a personal relationship with Jesus is like falling backwards into a big down comforter."

Susie Case, Age 32, Housewife,
New York City

"I HAVE AN image of God as a guy in high top sneakers with his feet up on a desk with his head turned away from the monitor that's keeping track of our universe—it does seem that he has his attention elsewhere."

Fred Navarro, Age 24, Student,
Washington, D.C.

I can see how it might be possible for a man to look down upon the earth and be an atheist, but I cannot believe how he could look up into the heavens and say there is no God.

Abraham Lincoln

"BECAUSE our prayers before dinner were silent, I thought, for the longest time, that silence was God and God was silence. When I sat there with my head bowed in silence, I felt like I was sitting in God.

"As I grew up, I got a lot more talkative and longed for a spoken dialogue with God, but I had this deep feeling that there was no language powerful enough to penetrate God's great, silent, timeless indifference.

"That's when I began to think of God in terms of lesser local gods or guardians. They are beings slightly more powerful than us that try their imperfect best, when asked in a heartfelt and sincere way, at divine intervention. Now when I pray, I pray to a small Balinese icon that was blessed and given to me in Bali by a Balinese shaman. I always speak out loud and begin by asking for the easement of world pain, then zero in on the more personal, particular needs. When I pray, I have a clear image of that jolly, laughing shaman who gave me the icon. He had a wonderful gold-toothed laugh and the memory of his laughter is as healing for me as the touch of any lesser god could be.

"It's like what Martin Dysart, the psychiatrist in *Equus,* meant when he said, 'Look. Life is only comprehensible through a thousand local Gods.' "

Spalding Gray, Age 48, Writer/Performer,
New York City

I would have less wish to go to heaven if I knew that God would not understand a joke.

Martin Luther

"WHEN I THINK of God, I think of the many things He gave us. I also think of the possibilities of how the earth was formed. I've even wondered if there is more than one God. I also wonder where He came from. Does He keep us like pets? Does He ever strike people down? What happens to dead people? So many questions, so little solutions."

Joy-Lyn Gulley, Age 12,
Anchorage, Alaska

A baby is God's opinion that the world should go on.

Carl Sandburg

"WE BELIEVE in one Supreme Being, Aka-Ba-Da-Dia, the first maker, the creator of all things. The Creator is kind of a mystical being who works through animals or plants, through nature, the wind, the air, fire, water, and the earth. When we seek a vision, we go on a vision quest. We'll fast for maybe three or four days and pray for guidance at night. This is how we get close to the Creator. By meditating we listen to what He has to give us. His interpreter comes in the form of an animal or in the form of wind or rain, thunder, or even a bird. This personal messenger talks to you and guides you. We never see the Creator Himself, but we learn His wishes. This is the way that the Medicine Man reaches spirituality, by communicating with the messenger."

Dan Old Elk, Age 50, Crow Sundance Chief,
Hardin, Montana

"I THINK God is a spirit, and part of the message of Jesus that's really appealing to me is that spirit lives both outside of us and inside of us and unites us to other people. I think the reason I go to church Sunday after Sunday is that it is compelling and moving to be with a group of people in that way. We have something in common—that we really want to learn how to love each other better. There is something useful about having a common framework of prayer. It seems to sometimes help smooth over life's bumps."

Ellen Schell, Age 37, Nurse,
San Francisco, California

"THE WAY I think of God is that He's the father I never had because my father left my mother when I was one year old."

Tyrone McCrae, Age 12,
Anchorage, Alaska

"As a woman, I'm aware of the specific and special ways women have an opportunity to know God. In a unique way, we as women come closer to the creative process in childbirth than any other species. As a woman, carrying another human life and nurturing that life for nine months in my body and literally putting my life on the line in the delivery process—as only women do—is an experience that is closer to God than any one I know."

Mary Cunningham-Agee, Age 38, Executive Director,
The Nurturing Network, Inc.,
Boise, Idaho

"I do believe God is a man. I believe He's a supreme being. God has a dark complexion, coarse hair, and red eyes. He's very handsome. He sits back and observes everything. He thinks deeply about what happens."

Lorrie Jemerson, Age 18,
University of Arkansas,
Pine Bluff

"FOR ME, growing up in a Hasidic family, the central question was the Holocaust. My family— my aunts, uncles, parents—were survivors. For me, talking about God was always a problem because I not only had to accept a God, but I had to accept a God that let my cousins get gassed to death. I found this extremely difficult. I'd go to synagogue and sit next to one person who didn't believe in God because he'd lost his family in the concentration camps. When I got older, he told me, 'Look, I come here because this is what I'm familiar with, but I cannot believe in a God that let my children be gassed.' And the other man tells me that after losing his children he has to believe in God—otherwise life would be pointless. So any discussion of theology is a discussion now about a God that was able to stand by while His people were tortured. I stopped having an easy time praying and believing in any kind of traditional God when I was eighteen. While there might not be a God now, perhaps there will be one in the future."

Joshua Halberstam, Age 43, Adjunct Philosophy Professor,
New York University,
New York City

"GOD IS someone who is in love with me. Somebody who is utterly, utterly convinced of my worth and my value. God is someone who likes me and has been trying to get across to me in all kinds of different ways. In the New Testament, in the first letter of St. John, there is a little description which says, 'God is love.' I'm convinced of that, but I would turn it around and say wherever love is found, God is somehow present."

Jaime Madrid, Age 48, Teacher,
Saint Meinrad Seminary and School of Theology,
Saint Meinrad, Indiana

"I THINK God does love us and I think He or She has a great compassion, but I believe that God has some faults just like everybody else. If He were all-loving and all-forgiving, we wouldn't be living in the world we live in right now and there would be peace. There wouldn't be fighting. There wouldn't be hunger or anything like that. I think God is overwhelmed by what's going on."

Jacki Maher, Age 20, Student,
University of Montana,
Missoula

"My description of God is a man sitting in the sky in a high chair looking down at what He created thousands of years ago."

Porfidio Beras, Age 15,
New York City

Outside man and nature nothing exists, and the higher beings which our religious phantasies have created are only the fantastic reflections of our individuality.

Friedrich Engels

"I HAVE to ask then 'Who is Allah?' It's easier for me understand more about Allah when I contemplate his ninety-nine attributes. First, He is the 'Source of Mercy.' So I think of the most merciful, kind, and considerate people I can possibly think of. I know that their mercy is just a fraction of what Allah has. Allah is also the Compassionate One, the Holy One, the Ruler. . . . Again, what I can imagine is only a fraction of His essence."

Jeanette Hablallah, Age 40, Teacher,
Lombard, Illinois

I believe in the sun even when it isn't shining. I believe in love even when I am alone. I believe in God even when He is silent.

Jewish refugee, World War II, Poland

"**I**N PUBLIC communal worship, I say Father, Son, and Holy Spirit but I never think of God that way personally. I say, 'the One whom Jesus calls Father.' I say the Lord's Prayer and I say the Creed and I say the Gloria Patrai and I lead that in worship because my people have always said those things. But God, for me, is not masculine only—but masculine and feminine. I prefer words such as 'Great Spirit,' which the Cherokee nation uses, or Master of the Universe, which is Hasidic. I also prefer the 'Eternal One,' a name I use when I worship in the synagogue of my choice and I have one! At my synagogue, that's what we say; we don't say 'Lord' because that is too human in its connotation."

Minka Shura Sprague, Age 37, Episcopal Deacon and
Professor, New York Theological Seminary,
New York City

"WHEN I think of God, I feel a certain security within myself because I know where my final destination will be."

Carla Guy, Age 27, YMCA Program Director,
Miami, Florida

"IT SEEMS to me that God is a convenient invention of the human mind. We are aware of our own ignorance and so we find refuge in a hypothetical being who knows everything. We are aware of our own weakness and so we find refuge in a hypothetical being who is all-powerful and who will take care of us out of a generalized benevolence. By imagining a God, then, human beings avoid having to do anything about their own ignorance and helplessness and this saves a lot of trouble."

Isaac Asimov, Age 70, Writer,
New York City

"IN LINGUISTIC terms, I think of God as a verb, not a noun. I think of Jesus as a metaphor, a mythic image, as well as an historical person who had profound inner experiences. For me, worship of Jesus as God is a form of idolatry. It's getting stuck on the image, instead of what lies beyond. And though images stir the memory of God, God, to me, is a mystery that is unspeakable and beyond the image."

Joe Wakefield, Age 45, Jungian Analyst,
Austin, Texas

"SOME PEOPLE don't like to call Buddhism a religion because of the fact that it doesn't have a central figure or a creator called God. For us religion is not God. Buddhism is a system of liberating oneself from suffering—cultivating and developing morality, concentration, and wisdom through meditation."

Henepola Gunaratana, Age 63, Buddhist Priest,
High View, West Virginia

"**G**OD'S PRESENCE helps me understand what life is all about. Humankind's ultimate question is not about power or wealth, but it is, 'What is the meaning of life?' It's that ability to understand what some call Buddha, what others call a higher power, and what I call Jesus Christ that gives me a feeling that I'm not alone and that there is someone more important than me that gives my life meaning."

Jeb Magruder, Age 55, Former Aide to President Nixon
and a minister, First Christian Church,
Columbus, Ohio

"**H**E HAS LEFT no record whatsoever of his existence in history other than hearsay several generations removed. There are no eyewitnesses' testimony to his life and even though he's claimed to be the Messiah by some, that claim rests on untrustworthy evidence that if—applied to anyone else—would not hold up in a court of law."

Gordon Stein, Editor,
The Encyclopedia of Unbelief,
Cranston, Rhode Island

"WHEN PEOPLE say not to question God 'cause it's wrong, they're wrong. It never hurts to question something we don't know. All you are doing is wanting to know God in your heart."

Eva Frances Santos, Age 15,
New York City

A thousand creeds have come and gone,
But what is that to you or me?
Creeds are but branches of a tree
The root of love lives on and on.

Ella Wheeler Wilcox

"In THE WEEKS after I yielded myself to the Lord, I felt bliss, an elevated feeling of 'good.' I felt God and I felt His direction. What happened over the course of eight years was that the church became less about God and more about the minister. He preached about salvation and yielding to God, knowing God and His grace, responding to God. But over time, he began to have this vision of salvation for the world. He seemed to no longer be guided by God Himself. . . . Everyone got really afraid because we'd met God in this church and had such powerful experiences and now it had evolved into something else. Experiences petered out, disintegrated—depending on how strong they were. It was hard to believe that God would have saved us in this context. Now I barely know what to call God or how to talk to Him."

Tony, Age 37, Former Christian Cult Member,
Farmington, Maine

Man is a god in ruins.

Ralph Waldo Emerson

"ANYBODY can say they found God. It's a personal experience they're talking about. The problem is with any human statement is that it's in a context and the context can always be examined. If the context doesn't reflect the high purposes and the high values and claims that the person is making about their experiences of God, then you've got a problem."

Joe Szimhart, Age 42, Deprogrammer,
Sante Fe, New Mexico

No one has ever died an atheist.

Plato

"ONCE I DREAMT what it must feel like to be God. At the time, I had been doing a lot of work with electronic music. That night I dreamt that I was a sine wave. I actually felt what it was like to be this rather abstract energy. It later occurred to me that I could have just as easily become a daisy or a door or a rock or a cat. I realized that being unencumbered by a human body, you have a whole different perception of things. This is where I muck it up a bit because now when I talk about it I'm interpreting the experience as 'Brian' would. When I was that sine wave, I was not tied to a 'body consciousness.' I was just a sine wave, pure and simple. That's what I think God is. Energy that is totally conscious of being everything—a sine wave, a speck of dust, a thought, you, me, whatever—but all at the same time."

Brian Mitchell,
Age 32, Actor and Musician,
Sherman Oaks, California

"IMAGINE THIS: Papa Smurf, Vanity Smurf, Happy Smurf, Baby Smurf. God is Papa Smurf and he looks down on these Smurfs and he sees them and he knows you have to go through the son to get to the father. Everything I do, I do in Jesus' name. When you take two steps toward Papa Smurf, he'll take twelve steps toward you."

Reverend Run Love of RUN-D.M.C.,
Age 24, Rap Musician,
New York City

My atheism, like that of Spinoza, is true piety towards the universe and denies only gods fashioned by men in their own image, to be servants of their human interests.

George Santayana

"THE WORD 'God' is probably one of the most misused words in the English language. I'll tell you one thing though. I am confused. If there is a God, why does he (or she) permit evil in this world? Why does he allow so many people to go through life feeling as though they're living in an unstable air mass? Are there any guarantees that he hears us if and when we pray? Is AIDS a special curse from him? Does he condemn couples for failed marriages? Where is he right now? Does he carry a beeper? Do you think he is genuinely concerned about *you* and your life? Did he create man with the knowledge of all the problems man was going to generate? Does he read our *every* brain wave? (If he does, he's probably more confused than we are.) How could anyone claim that they know where heaven is if they've never been there? I bet if God were to make a surprise appearance on national television right now, he'd probably shock the world with the details of the way he operates!"

Suzanne Wasielewski, Age 25, Writer,
Justice, Illinois

"GOD, the creator of all. The One who listens and responds to our every request, but does not receive the same courtesy from us. He must be merciful because this world still survives . . . in spite of itself."

Margaret A. Bradley, Age 39,
Contract Administrator,
Greenbelt, Maryland

Give me the benefit of your convictions if you have any, but keep your doubts to yourself, for I have enough of my own.

Johann Wolfgang von Goethe

"A WORD talking about God is very much like a finger pointing at the moon. It's not the moon; it's just a finger. A thousand names exist in Vishnu Hinduism, and ninety-nine in Islam and all of them are the names of the unnamable. Each name represents a different facet of God and when you put them all together they still don't represent the totality. It is not something that can be conceptualized. God is not a concept. It is beyond concept. Concepts just point in the direction. Like a diving board—you walk to the end of it then you dive in. In that sense you can't know God. You can be one with God or merge with God or know facets of God. It's the edge—where the form and the formless meet."

Ram Dass, Age 59, Spiritual Teacher,
San Anselmo, California

"I IMAGINE that God is like an older dark-skinned man who is always wearing nice slacks like a businessman—not a dirty brown toga like some people on TV always portray him."

Gene Rodriguez, Age 14,
Bronx, New York

"MY MORE general state and awareness of God is a state of communion with a loving presence, almost like never being alone. It's reassuring and it's guiding. Unlike a more transcendental experience of God, I don't lose my sense of self. I'm not egoless. I'm just there. It's like always being in the sunlight."

Nancy Sharpnack, Age 53,
Trance Channel for the Entity Etherion,
Albany, California

"IF I HAVE to believe in a trinity, the Father, Son, and Holy Ghost is more convincing to me than Liberty, Equality, and Fraternity."

Jonathan Silver, Age 51, Sculptor,
New York City

The God who gave us life, gave us liberty.

Thomas Jefferson

"I'M NOT A person who reads the Bible day and night. I don't go to church every single Sunday. To some people that means my faith is not strong, but it is. I love God. People think to have a strong faith you have to worship God. Sure, I worship God, but not in the way you think. He is a friend who I tell things to, like things I won't tell anyone else. I feel He is the best pal someone could have. When I move, He is always there to talk to. If all my other friends I like are mad at me, He won't be. He's a true friend who I love."

Shannon Person, Age 13,
Woodstock, Illinois

In the music, in the sea, in a flower, a leaf, in an act of kindness . . . I see what people call God in all these things.

Pablo Casals

"PRAYER IS the channel or the conduit for me. I think that prayer is quite possibly one of the most powerful forces known to me and to humankind. Coincidences seem to be God's way of remaining anonymous. Having a relationship with God is something I have to work at, like getting in shape or doing my job properly. My relationship with God did not fall out of the sky, but now I understand that I am a spiritual creature, and by allowing that spirit to be fed, I have a friendship with God. And it's funny because the more I get to know God and presumably get closer to God, the less I know—and the more powerful and mysterious and comical my definition of God becomes."

Steve Haweeli, Age 35, Bartender,
New York City

Which is it, is man one of God's blunders or is God one of man's?

Friedrich Nietzsche

"**Y**OU KNOW, I hear so many people pray that we need to serve the poor and serve the hungry and serve the lonely and serve the depressed. But we can't do that until we love the poor, and love the depressed, and love the lonely. We need to love. Christ came to Earth and who did He work with? He worked with the poor and the lepers. I'm not Christ but I have Christ in my heart. People ask me how I can work with AIDS patients. Who did Christ work with?"

Jim Sichko, Age 22, Student,
Orange, Texas

The Word is living, being, spirit, all verdant greening, all creativity. The Word manifests itself in every creature.

Hildegard of Bingen

"LIVING IS knowing God. I can only conclude that all life and death is miraculous. I am awed by it. I feel humbled by it. Everything I do in life is an offering. . . . An essential awareness of one's life process is the worship of God—because that means giving up concern about what other people have thought, are thinking, or will think. The elimination of fear is a process that takes place with the growth and awareness of the miraculous nature of life and death. And so, minding your own business as intensely as possible is an act of worship."

Olga Bloom, Age 70, President, Barge Music,
Fulton Ferry Landing,
Brooklyn, New York

"WHAT WE usually think of as reality is a frame that is fit over reality. The ultimate reality is a web-work of the relationships among all the possibilities. Every possibility is contained in the web of ultimate reality. It is a scientific fact that the wider the range of scope, the more probable the improbable will happen. So in the ultimate reality, all possibilities exist within one another in the web of relationships. This is true for completely opposite possibilities. This web of possibilities can be called God. For God, all things are possible."

Frank Moore, Age 43,
Shamanistic Performance Artist,
Berkeley, California

Whatever the queer little word means, it means something we can none of us quite get away from, or at; something connected with our deepest explosions.

D. H. Lawrence

"For the first ten years of my life, God was an ambiguous, spiritual being somewhere out above the clouds. Upon receiving His son Jesus Christ as my personal Lord and Savior while a college sophomore, God became my most intimate and personal friend. For thirty years, He has been my strength, my life, my hope, and everything good that is in the universe. I consult Him through prayer many times every day. I could not live one moment without Him."

Jerry Falwell, Age 56, Pastor,
Thomas Road Baptist Church,
Lynchburg, Virginia

If the concept of God has any validity or any use, it can only be to make us larger, freer and more loving. If God cannot do this, then it is time we got rid of Him.

James Baldwin

"To me, God is a spirit without physical form, unchanging, not a God who sits on a throne, writes sins in a book, and dispenses punishments. The world (universe) is ruled by laws, not God's caprice. We get no more nor no less than we deserve of the positive things in life. Eventually, possibly after many lifetimes, we will be perfected like Jesus—our way-shower—who was not God's only son.

"We are missing the boat if we think Jesus took away our sins or can singlehandedly save us. The world seems to be full of people who are like ships without rudders. The orthodox churches (I was a member for over fifty years, with strict attendance at Mass) have missed what Jesus taught. We are responsible for our own salvation. No church can save or condemn us."

John A. Devine, Age 58,
Retired Cartographer,
St. Louis, Missouri

"**I**'VE BEEN asked this same question on a lot of tests in the classroom, but I tended to go by what the teacher wanted to hear, not what I really believed. When I think of God, I always manage to relate the word to death. Yes, I've learned that God is loving and I truly believe this. I pray every night, but 'death' is the first word that pops into my mind when I am asked this question."

Germaine Denis, Age 15,
Queens, New York

Man is born broken; he lives by mending. The Grace of God is the glue.

Eugene O'Neill

"THE TRADITIONAL Hebrew word 'YHWH' has no vowels and is conventionally translated as 'Lord' in Jewish prayer books. In Hebrew, people usually—in order to avoid pronouncing these letters—use the euphemism 'Adonai.' We felt very uncomfortable with that understanding of how to deal with those four letters. In translation, 'Adonai' is transcendant, 'up there,' domination-oriented—rather than immanent, community-focused, and androgynous. One day I discovered a powerful and authentic way of dealing with the four letters and that was to pronounce it without any vowel sounds. The word came out like Yyyyhhhhwwwwhhh—just a breathing sound—which I realized was of course authentically and correctly the 'real' name of God. Breathing is a powerful metaphor for God. God is truly the breath of life."

Arthur Waskow, Age 56,
Director of The Shalom Center,
Philadelphia, Pennsylvania

"WE SEE glimpses of God's love when our humanity gets the best of us, when we just want to give up and question: Are you there? Why am I existing? And at these times, the spirit within you just wells up and gives you that answer. It's the answer I got when my eighteen-year-old daughter died last year. It was either that or throw it all out the window. There was nothing that I could have done, no religion I could have learned that would have sustained me through such a tragedy. It had to come from the outside into me and it did. That's God's grace. It's so evident, yet so intangible. We can't grab it, but we can sense it. Those of us who ask for it, get it. That's the reality of God."

Nick De Marco, Age 43,
Coordinating Director, Pierre Cardin, U.S.A.,
New York City

"I'M SURE you've heard the statement, 'We are just a dream in God's mind.' Well, I think that God is just a dream in our minds. It is something people choose to believe in because they simply need to. I have chosen not to believe foremost in God, but to believe in the power of my own mind."

April Poitra, Age 15,
Belcourt, North Dakota

An atheist's most embarrassing moment is when he feels profoundly thankful for something, but can't think of anybody to thank for it.

Mary Ann Vincent

"I'M STRUGGLING with what God means to me and I've never felt so alone. Sometimes I wish that everything would just resolve itself or dissolve. My confidence in everything goes down. I feel a lot less supported. Some people ask me, 'Are you religious?' and I say, 'No, but I'm spiritual.' But then when I'm alone, I wonder, 'Spiritual towards what?'"

Margaret Kim, Age 20,
Clark University,
Worchester, Massachusetts

"GOD IS LIKE the light I turn on in my room. He lets me see what's there."

An Eight-year-old Girl,
Princeton, New Jersey

"NEW AGE people think that they are God. They think everything is God. Whereas we have a God: He's up in heaven. He rules everything. He's a king."

Laurie Merkel, Age 19,
Liberty University,
Lynchburg, Virginia

God is a fire and you must walk on it . . . dance on it. At that moment the fire will become cool water. But until you reach that point, what a struggle, my Lord, what an agony!

Nikos Kazantzakis

"Before I became Muslim, I was confused about who God was. Because they kept saying that Jesus was the Son of God and that He was God. Then they'd say God the Father, God the Son and God the Holy Ghost. All these things were confusing to me because I'd be looking at three and they'd be saying 'one.' So I just gave up and stopped looking at it. So when I became Muslim and read the Holy Quran, I got a beautiful understanding of who God is and who Jesus is and who the prophets are and so on. It made me separate things but yet bring them back together in unity. Also, I'm very comfortable with the fact that all of the prophets are equal. There is no one prophet who is greater than another. They were all on the same mission: to bring the word of God to man."

Nuurah Amatullah Muhammad,
Age 59, Teacher,
Decatur, Georgia

What this country needs is a man who knows God other than by hearsay.

Thomas Carlyle

"IN THE CRAFT, one of the most important things we do is see Gods in each other. It's a very difficult task. But I think that it is one of the most extraordinary things a human being can do, to see God and Goddess in other human beings and to form partnerships and relationships based on that vision."

Deborah Lipp, Age 28, Wiccan Priestess,
Dumont, New Jersey

The existence of a Being endowed with intelligence and wisdom is a necessary inference from a study of celestial mechanics.

Isaac Newton

"I HAVE A sense of a personalized God, one that's kind of a Great Mother who is loving and nonjudgmental. And I also have a personalized image of a punitive God and he's always male. I don't like him very much. He's the one I get angry at. But the Mother God, I love her and I talk to her. She has a great power in my life. She's the force, the creative force, the enlightening force which I try to keep myself in line with. When I'm afraid, I talk about God. I touch into these moments, I feel more myself and more alive than any other time, and also less self-conscious than any other time.

"I think perfectionism equals death and therefore God must be imperfect. God must encompass light and dark. We have to accept our humanness and just allow ourselves to be pulled down that river, rather than fighting the current."

Roseanne Cash, Age 34, Musician,
Nashville, Tennessee

"ALLAH TO WHOM all praise is due is the mightiest and the most merciful. Allah (God) is not to be tampered with by the treacheries of technology or science."

Rahmel B. Richardson, Age 16,
New York City

"WHEN WE SEE the perfection in a child or lover or friend and when we let all the barriers and all the walls down, we're there in God together. God is the flowers, the trees, everything. It's all creation—as the Native Americans would say, 'the winged, the four-legged, all that flies, and all that swims.' God is completely forgiving and completely accepting, never ever judging. I sometimes have this feeling of God waiting in joyful anticipation of what we're going to do next on this journey back home into that place of truth—which is God."

Karla LaVoie, Age 44,
Educator/Counselor,
Asbury Park, New Jersey

"GOD IS THE electromagnetic field surrounding the earth out of which everything is composed."

Gabriel Green, Age 65,
President, Amalgamated Flying Saucer Clubs of America,
Yucca Valley, California

"I THINK GOD lives beyond space where just good dead people go. He has a beard and is very big. He has all kinds of boxes for body parts because that's how He can make people. He has personality in another box."

Amanda Innis, Age 8,
Princeton, New Jersey

"WHEN I SAY God, I mean Jesus Christ. Not for the sake of anyone's orthodoxy—far from it. Because in all my seventy-three years, I have found no more comprehensive, usable meaning.

"For much of my young life, I searched intellectually for what I felt secure in calling my concept of God. And then, through the life of a friend, almost by divine accident, I saw that my way of searching had been all wrong. I was making it all complex when God had, two thousand years ago, already made Himself plain in the person of Jesus Christ. At that moment, an ongoing opening began in me and it is still ongoing. After more than forty years, I am still convinced that if God did reveal Himself in Jesus Christ, I can put my eternal weight down upon that fact.

"If God is like Jesus, then we can all relax, knowing His full intentions toward us. I depend daily, not on some flailing preacher's idea of God, but on the person Himself. This is the Great Simplicity. Faith in God simply follows. Faith to me is the inevitable result of learning more and more of what God is really like.

"Jesus himself said, 'I and the Father are one.' Did He really know? Nearly half a century of conscious living with Him in both the bright and dark places is long enough to be sure. He did know. If God is like Jesus Christ, how can I not trust Him?"

Eugenia Price, Age 73, Writer,
St. Simons Island, Georgia

"A LONG TIME ago, when I was a nurse, I would see God in other people through their bravery, their suffering, and through their determination to live—knowing that they had a fatal disease or knowing that their child had a fatal disease. Also, I often see God when families interact with each other—when they are forgiving and loving and good to each other. That's God."

Joan Stiff, Age 58, Mayor,
Woodside, California

He who needs least is most like the Gods.

Socrates

"WHEN I THINK of God, it's pretty hard not to think of His son, Jesus Christ. God sometimes seems way out there and you're not really sure about Him, but when you focus on Jesus, you get a much clearer picture of what God is really like."

Tom Landry, Age 66,
Former Coach of the Dallas Cowboys,
Dallas, Texas

Nobody talks as constantly about God as those who insist that there is no God.

Heywood Broun

"In God, I feel my strength. God connects us to possibilities, to potential, to other people. God is that part of us that cares for a child that is starving in another country."

Colleen Ping, Age 25, Mother,
Ocean Grove, New Jersey

To know God and to live are the same thing. God is life.

Leo Tolstoy

"GOD IS sometimes forgotten in man's conquest for fortune and fame, ignored as another human or drug is relied on, often blamed for man's frailties, denied as man worships himself. In a moment of darkness, man cries out for help and comfort—'Oh God!' And in that moment, man acknowledges that presence of one more powerful than he."

Geri Guiney, Age 47, Nurse,
Chicago, Illinois

"I BELIEVE that when He wants someone to join Him, He will take him. My brother was killed in a car accident two weekends ago. I have never cried or hurt so much. But it makes me feel better to know that he was ready to be with God in heaven. I feel that my faith in God has helped me deal with this crisis. I loved my brother and I know that I will see him someday in heaven."

Mary, Age 14,
Old Greenwich, Connecticut

"GOD IS potential—if I want to draw on it. God works through an urge to grow, an urge toward perfection. I see what I call God working in people. When someone thinks something through and says, 'I've just got to do that better,' or 'This is what I need to look at,' that's the growth principle in people, being the best you can be. That's God at work . . . The spirit of God embodied in a human being is full of compassion; it's vulnerable to hurt—any way, anywhere. What does it mean to be close to God in the way that Jesus was close to God? What is the Christ spirit I personally experience? The spirit of God moves me, touches me. It's the spirit at the growing edge of my life. This has to do with being utterly true to yourself, with being human and not trying to 'be holy.' To use words as a litmus test was not what Jesus had in mind. To say that you have to believe in Christ in order to get to heaven is another crucifixion of what Christ was all about."

Marty Walton, Age 53,
General Secretary, Friends General Conference,
Philadelphia, Pennsylvania

"I HAD ALWAYS seen God as creator and man as the destroyer. Lately, though, I have come to understand God as the enabler, a quiet source of strength which supports me as I seek to be my best. Perhaps it is passé to want to improve the world; but the beat of God within me prompts me onward just the same."

Marlene A. D. Binkley, Age 33, Photographer/Teacher,
Chicago, Illinois

There are innumerable definitions of God because His manifestations are innumerable. They overwhelm me with wonder and awe and for a moment stun me. But I worship God as Truth only. I have not found Him, but I am seeking after Him. I am prepared to sacrifice the things dearest to me in pursuit of this quest.

Mahatma Gandhi

"WHEN I WAS younger, I had a strong aversion to the use of the word 'God.' In fact I avoided it and I avoided people who spoke about God. I attended a powerful workshop with a Huichol Indian shaman who was 104 years old. He introduced me to his culture's Deer God. I got really intrigued with this Deer God and it sort of got to me on a personal level. After the workshop, I bought a bag from the shaman which had been used to gather peyote and this bag had deer woven into it. At home alone, I began getting images of the deer, and at the same time, live deer started wandering into my back yard. I meditated every day and began talking to the Deer God. Very slowly, over time, I found myself talking to the Deer God, saying 'Deer God' this and 'Deer God' that. One day I noticed that I was saying 'Dear God.' It was so powerful that I had to laugh. It was like I tricked myself into the use of that 'word.' It snuck in the back door. I've been in love with God ever since."

Martha Powers, Librarian,
Sherwood, Oregon

"THERE IS a space where there is nothing. We don't know what is there. To me, it's a kind of black hole and God is that black hole. It's a blackness of nonunderstanding."

John Myers, Age 36, Biologist,
Bernardsville, North Carolina

"I'M JUST A light bulb, but there's a power line, His name is God and I don't try to take His job. I just try to be the bulb. I don't try to be the source of power. Oh, listen, it's a Duracell battery, just never runs out."

Mother York, Age 65,
Director of a "Jailhouse Ministry"
in the Cook County Jail,
Chicago, Illinois

"**I** THINK THE whole quest for oneness, for spiritual connection in the world, is that quest to see the divine in one another. Sometimes I see God in my autistic child because he's not of this world and yet he's partly of this world. Sometimes we connect in ways that seem of this world —in intelligence and exuberance and joy and play and celebration. Other times, we connect in ways that words can't describe. I look in his eyes and he looks in mine. I know that we're present together, connected. I can't explain it, but it's at that time, I see God in my son. I see the divinity."

Jim Autry, Age 57, Poet and President,
Magazine Group, Meredith Corp.,
Des Moines, Iowa

"**T**HE WILLINGNESS of people to share, their ability to love one another, to work for the common good, to sacrifice for one another: that is God."

Rosa Maria Royo, Age 26,
YMCA Program Director,
Miami, Florida

"GOD IS a psychological phenomenon. It doesn't make any difference whether or not God exists because the effect of belief on people's minds is the same."

Kendra Willson, Age 17,
Student, Harvard University,
Cambridge, Massachusetts

In my most extreme fluctuations I have never been an atheist in the sense of denying the existence of God.

Charles Darwin

"IT SEEMS TO ME that our understanding of what or who God is proceeds or happens simultaneously as we understand who we are. I don't think we learn one without the other. So as our own selves begin to emerge and we begin to understand the self in all its parameters—as deeply as that means—then the 'Face of God' is likely to emerge."

Laurie Sackler, Age 39, Housewife,
Brooklyn, New York

"I WAS SITTING and praying one day and I saw myself as a seventeen-year-old girl and I was following Christ on a beach. I was saying, 'You won't believe what's happened now,' and I got so excited about everything that was going on in my life and how well my imagery sessions were going. I ran up in front of Him and I was standing in front of Him waving my hands in the air, talking. Then I stopped dead in my tracks and stopped talking. Then in this image, I started to laugh and He looked at me and laughed too and said . . . No, He didn't say anything. It was so obvious that He knew everything and I was acting as if He didn't know what happened, as if He wasn't a part of everything, all of it. Then He said that He was really happy for me and reminded me to walk with Him side by side. He told me that whenever I do work of the spirit, to do it through Him. He said if I stay with Him, I won't get lost or do harm or get caught up in myself. At that moment, His words silenced me and, again, rejuvenated me. I felt that God was saying, 'Walk with me, but if you get too tired, I'll carry you on my back,' and I thought of the words 'in Him, with Him, and through Him.' "

Casey Flynn, Age 39,
Works with Creative Imagery and Healing,
St. Paul, Minnesota

Things are to be used and God is to be loved. We get into trouble when we begin to use God and love things.

Jay Kesler

"**I** TRY TO let go and let the Lord. That's why I'm here today. I thank God that He kept me over the night and I thank God for all the ones in the world He kept over the night. He didn't have to keep us, but He did, because He loves us. If we love a little more and suffer a little more for one another, things would be a little better."

Minnie V. Baker, Age 85, Great-grandmother,
Rochester, New York

A man can no more diminish God's glory by refusing to worship Him than a lunatic can put out the sun by scribbling the word "darkness" on the walls of his cell.

C. S. Lewis

"HINDUISM, the way I perceived it to be when I was a little girl growing up in India, involved a lot of ritualism. I had no patience with it, and it had no meaning for me since I did not understand the meaning of and the reasoning behind all the ritual. In our house, half the day was spent on rituals—God this and God that. So I sort of got turned off. Years later, after I got married and had children, I realized that there is a God. The beauty and mystery of Nature opened my eyes to this. Then away from the din of my family and all the rituals, the gurus started to make some sense. They are superior human beings who have attained levels of perfection which I certainly haven't or will not attain for a while. They are God's messengers, here to teach us how to achieve oneness with God and overcome the cycle of rebirth."

Uma K. Desai, Age 49, Financial consultant, Lawrenceville, New Jersey

"WE BELIEVE God is supernatural. Faith is believing without seeing. So have faith and gain eternal happiness. No mortal being can begin to comprehend God. So why try?"

Emelia Barley, Age 63, Retired cashier,
Schertz, Texas

"WHEN WE talk to God, we're praying. When God talks to us, we're schizophrenic."

Lily Tomlin, Age 51, Actress,
Los Angeles, California

We can act *as if* there were a God; feel *as if* we were free; consider Nature *as if* she were full of special design; lay plans *as if* we were to be immortal; and we find then that these words do make a genuine difference in our mortal life.

William James

"WHEN MY father died of cancer, I said silently, 'Thank You, God, for not letting him suffer anymore.' When my mother died of old age, I said silently, 'Thank You, God, for not letting her suffer anymore.' When my husband died suddenly in a car accident, I asked God why did this happen and why did You take him from me? I didn't expect an answer to the last loss as He does not give answers. But I knew God was there to hear me in my suffering and it was a comfort to be able to talk to Him through the many hours of tears and crying. He was my source of comfort through a very difficult time."

Anita Stein, Age 60, Secretary,
Skokie, Illinois

"THE POWER to accept what God means for me is recognizing that God is the Lord of time when my idea of timing doesn't agree with his."

Lillian Dvorak, Age 55, Secretary,
Berwyn, Illinois

"GOD IS from whom we may not get what we want, but do find peace with what we get."

Marilyn D. White, Age 58, Jeweler,
Chicago, Illinois

"WHEN I WAS a little kid, I had a vision. I was sitting in my favorite tree and wondering about God. How could it be that God was inside of me? How could that be true? So I started looking at myself and thinking of all the planets and other worlds and other people. I decided that I was a cell in God's body and that we're all cells for that matter, one part of a larger whole working together or against ourselves as a species."

Petey Stevens, Age 45, Executive Director,
Heartsong Center for Expanded Perception,
Albany, California

"He's sort of unexplainable. Everyone knows the textbook definitions: all knowing, all loving, omnipotent, all powerful, supreme being, heavenly creator. This is the problem. This is why kids or even adults sometimes can't relate to Him. People aren't comfortable with the image. They don't want to be in the same room with a guy like that, much less be with Him and love Him. I see God as a friend, a guy I hang out with, a poker buddy, a fishing pal, someone you can relax with. In all seriousness, I can picture myself kicking back with God and having a cold one. Really, I mean it."

Rich Popovic, Age 15,
Yonkers, New York

"I'm a Christian and I see God everywhere people want Him to be. If you are in that part of God's kingdom that says Mohammed is the interface between you and God and you want to have a conversation with God, He's there for you. He's there for us all."

Duwayne Lundgren, Age 53,
Deputy Director, U.S. Army Intelligence Agency,
Falls Church, Virginia

"GOD TEACHES me lessons during the workday. Being in construction, I've cleared lots, done electrical work, built roofs, painted. Clearing the lot can be boring and time-consuming. But all that foundation work was to be done, not only on the job but in our hearts. I've worked on projects where the foundation wasn't level. And once you get to the second story, you've got to go back and make all these adjustments. I really see that God wants me to take the time to build a strong foundation for Him in my heart."

Jim Ryan, Age 24, Carpenter,
Panama City, Florida

Prayer does not change God, but it changes the one that offers it.

Søren Kierkegaard

"WHEN I'M at a concert, I think of God. It amazes me that people could be created to compose and play music. Last night, my husband and I heard Mahler's Second Symphony. When the John Oliver Choral Group performed with the Boston Symphony, God was there. I felt as if angels were singing. It was very ethereal. To me that was better than going to Temple and praying. At the concert, inside my own self, I gave thanks to God for creating something so wondrous."

Trudi Mishara, Age 57, Housewife,
Lexington, Massachusetts

"GOD IS what humankind turns to when life overwhelms. To me, God is everything. God is all."

Sonny Rollins, Age 59,
Tenor Saxophone Player,
Germantown, New York

"GOD IS always willing to enter into a running dialogue or debate with man. This is a tradition of 'talking up' in Jewish history. When I think of Abraham 'hondling' with God about Sodom and Gomorrah, I think of Woody Allen or Neil Simon. Meeting God on your own terms humanizes God. It makes Him more accessible. So it's hard for Jews to be fundamentalists—even the most pious Jews. When I was a little boy, I was told by my teachers that I had two hands: one for text and one for commentary. We believe that there is something lurking beyond the words. Text is the tip of the iceberg and I can't get too committed to it or my views will be narrow. It invigorates me to know that I have to be actively involved in discovering God."

Moshe Waldoks, Age 40, Humorist,
Boston, Massachusetts

"**E**UPHEMISM for an ancient hierarchy used through generations to control people's actions. Evolving into modern-day laws and values. Eschewed by many until death approaches. Revered more by poor, sick, uneducated, elderly, and traditional people as a bonding element (with no physical proof of existence) in hopes of an 'afterlife.' "

Les Jones, Age 63, Railway Control Operator,
Munster, Indiana

"**F**ISH IN the ocean don't doubt its existence; they live in it. God is like that, the ground of all beings, being itself. A fish out of water dies. A man apart from God ceases to be man. He may continue to breathe but he is dead."

William Graham Cole, Age 72, Educator,
Chicago, Illinois

"WHEN WE experience awe, we come close to feeling the presence of God. Like the state of awe, when we come to know God we sense the presence of something within and apart from us that is infinite. We are not afraid of this feeling. We delight in it. God transcends our humanness, much as awe transcends our normal range of emotions."

Frederick A. Gougler, Age 36, Bank Officer,
Northfield, Illinois

"IF THERE is anything you care enough about for which you would give up your life, then you know what God means. Otherwise forget it. Definitions, scripture, or going to 'church' will not help. God isn't found there, but only in life—a life that's lived, not just passed through."

Reinhard Plaut, Age 56, Architect,
Des Plaines, Illinois

"**I**'VE STOPPED questioning the meaning of life at the most fundamental level. Before, I thought life was meaningless. I might be having a good day-to-day existence, but I didn't feel as if there was any real meaning to life. I always felt like it didn't matter if I got hit by a truck today or tomorrow. Now that I believe in God, I don't have that total emptiness I had before. I have more hope."

Heather Evans, Age 31, Entrepreneur,
New York City

What pattern connects the crab to the lobster and the orchid to the primrose and all four of them to me? And to you?

Gregory Bateson

"WHEN PEOPLE ask me if I've been 'born again,' I smile slyly and say 'yes' and what I mean is that I've been active in a group of women in the Bay Area who are struggling to establish what women's spirituality is. We are a group of Christians, Buddhists, and Jews and Wiccan witches. We go around the calendar year and share rituals with each other. Once we were working on a witches' initiation ritual and I was very uncomfortable because I thought, 'This is *so* pagan.' At this time I was just getting over the end of a pretty obsessive relationship so I decided to look at the ritual as a way of finally leaving that person. So I thought, 'Okay, the end of this. Just do it.' I was vowing to change my behavior and halfway through the ceremony I heard a voice saying to me, 'You've lived your whole life by male standards and you have no idea what it is to live by women's standards, let alone your own.' The voice was God's presence and that's how I was 'born again.'"

Nancy Chinn, Age 50,
Artist-in-Residence, Pacific School of Religion,
Berkeley, California

"**G**OD IS the answer to the unfathomable."

Nancy Namest, Age 31, Office Manager,
Chicago, Illinois

"**I** THINK that we've all been given a sort of map to a city. One person lives to the north. One person lives to the east. Nobody lives in exactly the same place. Well, if everyone was given the exact same map to get to that same point, everyone but one person would be extremely lost. As we get closer to a sort of universal harmony and as we get more in tune, I think the squabbling stops, because then everybody agrees, 'Oh yeah, I understand your map.'"

Kort Falkenberg III, Age 37,
Film and Video Director,
North Hollywood, California

There is a god-shaped vacuum in every man that only Christ can fill.

Augustine

"IT'S LIKE A hologram. God is the spirit behind every one of us—although we think of ourselves as separate beings. Like a hologram, His total image is in each of us. Each fractionated part still shows a picture of the whole."

John Gale, Age 44, Mechanical Engineer,
Columbia, South Carolina

To define God is to limit Him. Still it seems inevitable that man should do that in order to get some edge to which his mind may cling.

Heywood Broun

"MY VIEW of God changes because my relationship with God changes, and just like any relationship, there are times when we're close and dear and intimate and there are times when you know it's sort of like routine and, at other times, sort of has negative emotions, anger, fear, resentment. There are days that I'm annoyed at God and I say, 'Look, I don't want have to deal with you today.' There are other days when we're sort of just sitting around having coffee—so to speak. There is also a certain amount of unfinishedness in my relationship with God. And I like it that way. I mean, suppose you and your best friend were to sit down and said the way our relationship is today is the way it's going to be forty years from now. That would be boring."

Terrence J. Mulry, Age 37, Writer,
Ridgewood, New Jersey

The awful thing is that beauty is mysterious as well as terrible. God and the devil are fighting there, and the battlefield is the heart of man.

Fyodor Dostoyevski

"GOD IS something you think about when you think about your death. I agree with John Lennon: 'God is the name we give to our pain.' I saw a glimpse of God when I saw my daughter Juliet and son Adam come out of my wife's body. Then I lose my sense of God when I see torture and starvation. Why would She allow it? To me the idea of God is wishful thinking—that a nice girl exists who will make things O.K. I want to believe in God because I want to go on living after I die."

Jerry Rubin, Age 52, Entrepreneur,
New York City

If you would be a real seeker after truth, it is necessary that at least once in your life you doubt, as far as possible, all things.

René Descartes

"GOD IS the great teacher who comes to us in our dreams as friends, guides, and allies. God is the universal subconsciousness. I believe we are on this planet to learn, this is a planet of lessons. Basically, that's why we're here. Jesus Christ was a very strong teacher and had a great many gifts. He channeled the Christ spirit and the Christ spirit is a very strong spirit, a spirit of healing. The Christ Consciousness is the most empowering, peaceful, centered, loving feeling I've ever experienced in my life. It's what you call joy and sorrow at the same time. It is so overwhelming. If every person on this planet could share that feeling simultaneously for one second, this planet would be healed."

Kathy Korpi, Age 35, Artists' Manager,
West Bloomfield, Michigan

Yes, my voices were of God; my voices have not deceived me.

Joan of Arc

"GOD IS in your heart guiding you—even if you don't recognize it. It's as if you had a diamond and you buried it in dirt. There'd still be a diamond in there: you just wouldn't be able to see it."

Christina Adams, Age 37, Screenwriter,
Sherman Oaks, California

I believe that a triangle, if it could speak, would in like manner say that God is eminently triangular, and a circle that the divine nature is eminently circular; and thus would every one ascribe his own attributes to God.

Baruch Spinoza

"MY PERSONAL belief is that yes, there is a God and God is the only God according to God's word—the Bible. But by accepting Christ as my personal savior, He lives in me. And if I pay attention to the teaching of the Scripture, then my life ought to exhibit those teachings. To say that I'm a Christian financial advisor is misleading. The proper term is financial advisor who follows biblical guidelines in the application of my profession. God's word is dependable, accurate, and always true, but we have to exercise discipline and patience to let His word work in our life. I think it's so important for a person to look at the management of their finances from a type of biblical perspective because it keeps one out of trouble. It gives you a feeling of comfort and safety in managing your financial affairs."

Don Ward, Age 55, Financial Advisor,
Fresno, California

"WHEN I TALK about God, I'm usually talking about John Barleycorn, the Green God, the spirit of all vegetation. He's the Jack in the Green. He comes up in the springtime and grows wise in the summer. He's reaped in the fall and we bake His body into bread and eat it and this is the origin of the Christian Eucharist as well as many Pagan festivals and even the song 'John Barleycorn.' When I speak of the Goddess, I don't mean it in the monotheistic sense. I realize that a lot of women's spirituality groups have basically just simply used the word 'Goddess' to replace 'God.' To me, that kind of Goddess is just God in drag."

Morning Glory Zell, Age 41, Histologist,
Ukiah, California

"God to me is the sum total of all the energy that I see flying around. I try to make my entire being a prayer. My prayers stretch as far as the farthest edge of our conception of the universe to whatever crawls out from under a rock when I move it. I think God is it, all, everything, the good and the bad, the laughter and the tears, everything. So when I pray, that's what I'm praying to, and I call it by everything that I was taught as a kid. All those Jesus images and Michelangelo images come to mind. And sometimes it's Buddha, sometimes Mohammed, sometimes Gandhi. I always put a face on God, but my soul knows that the face isn't God. Putting a face on God is a human trick to make God more accessible."

Graham Nash, Age 47, Musician,
Encino, California

"WHEN WE say God, we mean the infinitely pure, perfect, and eternal spirit who is the beginning and the end of all creation, who is the unfulfilled longing in each of us, and to whom each of us is ultimately accountable for what we do and fail to do."

John A. Yeabower, Age 58, Retired Air Force pilot,
Annapolis, Maryland

Belief in God is acceptance of the basic principle that the universe makes sense. That there is behind it an ultimate purpose.

Carl Wallace Miller

"THE MARVELOUS thing for me about God is that the God concept is something that works for people regardless of what stage of spiritual development or inner knowing they are at. The simplest person with very little capabilities or intelligence can have a concept of God and so can the person who is as enlightened as we can imagine. The God concept is as multilevel as you can imagine. This is not true of other notions in our world.

"God is a very personal thing—which does not mean He is a person. It means that each person has the opportunity to devise his own notion of what is God to him. That's sacred. None of us has the right to take that away from anyone else —which is to say that if we do, we are transgressing on something pretty heavy."

William Kautz, Age 65, Executive Director,
The Center for Applied Intuition,
Fairfax, California

"SOME PEOPLE are able to describe or name God better than others. My sense is that everyone does it exquisitely for themselves and perfectly in their dreams. The best theologian is the source within. And there is no such thing as a bad dream. What seems to be a nightmare is nothing more than an urgent message. The myth that appeals to me the most is that we are all characters in God's dream, that we all exist in relation to one another in exactly the same structural fashion that our dream images exist in relation to our total personalities. So James Joyce is absolutely and technically correct when he says that history is a nightmare from which we are struggling to awake."

Jeremy Taylor, Age 43,
Unitarian Minister and Teacher,
Institute in Culture and Creation Spirituality,
Oakland, California

"**I** SUPPOSE I divvy God up. I mean, I have a Jesus that I can talk to, and there's a God which is sort of beyond me, but talking about it makes it smaller than what it is. I view God at different times in different ways. There are times when I can really feel a personal God and times when I can feel a God that is beyond personness. The times that I feel closest to God are usually when I've run out of answers."

Norma Harrington, Age 60, Retired Teacher,
San Francisco, California

Man is certainly stark mad. He cannot make a worm, and yet he will be making gods by the dozens.

Jean-Paul Marat

"THE JEWISH notion of God is not really explicit, perhaps because we do not believe that God ever took human form or walked the earth. When I try to speak about God, I think it is often to share my perplexity. I often cite the parable from a children's textbook about a little fish. One day he is swimming close to the surface when he hears somebody talking about the water—only he doesn't know what is meant by water. He wonders: 'Where is the water?' So he swims around and asks all the different fish, 'Where is the water?' but they don't know. Finally he finds the wisest fish in the ocean, who says, 'The water is all around you. The water is inside you. The water travels through you.' But the little fish just laughs and swims off. To this day he is still asking, 'Where is the water?' "

Robert Kirschner, Age 39, Rabbi,
Congregation Emanu-El,
San Francisco, California

"I SEE GOD as the sea. I think of people as bowls by the sea and we sit there and the sea pours into the bowl and it brings whatever it is that we're looking for. On a certain level, whatever we ask for we get. And it just goes in and out. When I need to be connected to that infinite intelligence, I try to imagine the tide going in and out. The direction we're looking for, the answer, the person, it will come to us like the tide. When I'm confused or uncertain about a decision I've had to make, I meditate. I've always gotten the answer. My ten-week-old son, Julian, is a perfect example of a meditation that manifested itself, because I just can't think of anything more perfect."

Catherine Tatge, Age 39, Documentary Film Producer,
New York City

"To me, God is an obstacle to rational thinking. Since there is no real evidence on how the universe came about, it's easy to say God created the heavens and the earth (and in seven days). Let's face it. God is the universal symbol for ignorance to those who can't or won't think for themselves."

Leonard Stanley, Age 65, Marketing Manager,
Silver Spring, Maryland

I would rather believe that God did not exist than believe that He was indifferent.

George Sand

"TRYING TO find God is like looking for an unlisted phone number—only much worse. People who aren't insiders don't have his number. They feel he is inaccessible. At least with the telephone company, you can call and rant and rave and invent a family emergency and they might give you the number. But no one can tell you how to find God.

"There is definitely a greater force that can screw people over, a main guy who controls the time clock. Also, God is certainly a man. It's a man's world. He's set it up so maleness controls. Don't misunderstand me. There's an advantage to being female. Females can see through maleness. But nature is wild and dangerous. It's very male to be aggressive and make people feel threatened. Human interaction is what softens and smooths and that comes from women."

Marian Salzman, Age 31, Media Executive,
New York City

"GOD IS not out there in the universe. The universe is in God."

Glendall Stilts, Age 71, Retired,
Florissant, Missouri

"GOD IS all that is good. I don't find God in a church any more than in a restaurant or shopping center. God is a kind word, a helping hand, forgiveness."

Joanne Stevenson, Age 56, Salesperson,
La Grange, Illinois

"GOD IS some sort of force. It's neither benign nor malignant and it just exists. I don't think that it's judgmental. It could probably care less about what we're doing in our lives. It just probably sees the overall results."

Susan Bryer, Age 20, Student,
Rensselaer Polytechnic Institute,
Troy, New York

"BACK WHEN I was active in my alcoholism, I had no feeling for God, no understanding of Him, no faith. I didn't have any kind of friendship with Him at all. I was in the Program for a couple of years before I started understanding God. AA and NA teach you how to live. A lot of the things they say will happen, do. I realized they started happening because I started to have faith in myself. And the reason I had faith in myself was because I had faith in a higher power. Once it started happening, I started looking into it on my own. I started accepting it more. Getting to know God has been a natural evolution. (And I'm not an AA moonie or a Big Booker. I haven't replaced one addiction with another. I'm just happy.)"

Sheila Carey, Age 36, Interior Designer,
Sun Valley, Idaho

Your cravings as a human animal do not become a prayer just because it is God you ask to attend them.

Dag Hammarskjöld

"God is not money or a new car. God is not a girlfriend or a special sunset. Money comes and goes. A car rusts and breaks down. A girlfriend, you can spend special moments with, but she's not always there when you need her. A sunset is lost in the distance—just when it's at it peak. The point I'm trying to make is that people of our society worship the things that will not always be with them. But God will always be with us. God isn't concerned about what kind of car we have or where our dad works. He doesn't break away from us if we move. God loves us for what we are, not for what others want us to be."

John Maguire, Age 16,
Chester, New York

The gods play games with men as balls.

Titus Maccius Plautus

"SINCE I asked Christ to be my Lord and Savior, there are still some peaks and valleys, but I am being operated on by the greatest Doctor of them all, so that all glory goes to Him."

Julius "Dr. J" Erving, Age 44,
Former Philadelphia 76er,
Philadelphia, Pennsylvania

I have lived a long time, sir, and the longer I live the more convincing proofs I see of this truth—that God governs in the affairs of men.

Benjamin Franklin

"GOD IS everything to me. I love the sport basketball, but I love God much more because without him, I would not have the energy or the skill to play ball. I am a very popular person. People look at me as if I don't need anybody. But they are very much mistaken."

Kendal H. Johnson, Age 16,
New York City

God is everything which is good, as I see it, and the goodness which everything has is God.

Julian of Norwich

"TEENAGE GOD

That God exists the world is not proof
But a metaphor for who She really is,
an unrestrained adolescent, showing off,
An excessive, exuberant, playful whiz,
Determined gamester with the quantum odds,
An ingenious expert in higher math—
This frolicsome and comic dancing God
Is charming and just a little daft.

Will God grow up? Will She become mature?
In the creation game announce a lull,
Her befuddled suppliants assure
A cosmos that is quiet, safe, and dull?
Can God be innocent of romance?
No Way! On with the multi-cosmic dance!"

(A sonnet on first having read *Physics, Philosophy and Theology* by Robert John Russell, William R. Stoeger, S.J., and George V. Coyne)

Andrew Greeley, Age 62,
Writer and Catholic Priest,
Chicago, Illinois

"SOMETIMES when I meditate, God comes up as my grandmother with a frying pan in her hand."

Ellie Shepardson, Age 53,
Attorney and Minister,
Berkeley, California

We say to ourselves, it would be very nice if there were a God, who was both creator of the world and a benevolent providence, if there were a moral world order and a future life, but at the same time it is odd that this is all just as we should wish it ourselves.

Sigmund Freud

"ALONG WITH being the All-powerful, the Living, Allah possesses limitless knowledge that encompasses everything. He is aware of the tiniest of particles. Nothing escapes His knowledge. He knows the numbers of the whirling stars and planets in the heavens, the grains of sand in the deserts of Earth, and the droplets of water in the oceans, rivers, and rain. He sees the worlds of life and things. His knowledge penetrates the past, the unknowns of the present, and the future, unbound by time or space or visibility. Knowing, the near and far, the big and small, is equal to Him. He knows what the hearts conceal and the truth of what people reveal."

Ahmad Zaki Hammad,
President, Islamic Society of North America,
Plainfield, Indiana

"MY GOD is that tremendous source of power that keeps everything in this huge and frantic world going and growing and orderly. When the pace and pressure of this world gets overwhelming, I meet Him most intimately, for He's the dad whose lap I've never outgrown. Whenever I curl up in His arms, I find comfort and love and peace."

Dan Smith, Age 36, School principal,
Woodstock, Illinois

"IF I AM the sail, God is the wind. If I am the cloud, God is the sky. If I am the roots, God is the tree. If I am the thought, God is the manifestation. If I am the sound, God is the word."

Bryce Bond, Age 61, Host of TV Show
"Dimensions in Parapsychology,"
New York City

"SOME DAYS He comes in the form of a phone call from a loving child just checking to see if Mother is all right. Other times, He appears as a neighbor administering a special favor. Sometimes, I have seen Him in the smile of a stranger who seems to have found the secret of having joy in a crazy world. I not only see Him in the good every day, but I see Him most when disaster strikes and friends you have never seen before are helping friends they have never met before. I had rather live believing He exists and die to find out He doesn't than to not believe and die, only to find out He does!"

Fern Daily, Age 57, Leasing Consultant,
Whitewater, California

Joy is the most infallible sign of the presence of God.

Teilhard de Chardin

"GOD IS the embodiment of unconditional love, wisdom, and strength. God is the source of energy which science has not yet been able to describe. It's the energy which flows through all creation. It's the love that cycles back through the universe over and over again."

Carol Madden, Age 30, Nurse,
Taos, New Mexico

It is easier to think of the world without a creator than of a creator loaded with all the contradictions of the world.

Simone de Beauvoir

"ONE OF the main teachings of siddha yoga is that God dwells within you as you. Some people get the Guru confused with God and it's very easy to do. You put so much into her. A true guru would never encourage that kind of thinking because it's detrimental. She is just there showing us how to do it for ourselves. She's just there giving us the awakening, giving us the key to unlock our hearts. But you have to be the one to put in the effort.

Mallorie Salomon, Age 22, Student,
Los Angeles, California

The energy of atheists, their tireless propaganda, their spirited discourses, testify to a belief in God which puts to shame mere lip worshipers. They are always thinking of God.

Fulton J. Sheen

"We GREET the sun because the sun gives us warmth and life. Somebody along the way said, 'These guys are worshiping the sun.' But we're not worshiping the sun, we just honor the sun by greeting it in the morning and we pray to the Creator. The Creator created the sun, the moon, the stars, Mother Earth. We have just one Creator. Though the Creator has no gender, we often refer to him as Great Spirit God or Grandfather.

"The Creator put things here for a purpose and that is why we respect the plants, the trees, and even the rock that's lying on the ground. Our forefathers don't teach us that the tree is there for the leaves to give off oxygen. It is up to us to see why the tree is there. In our teachings, they simply teach us to respect these things and to respect other people and other people's space. Our Creator cannot judge you. The Creator is there to guide you. But we have the 'other place' and that's where your spirit goes when your body is returned to the earth. And you don't have to be good to get there. It's just a place you are going to go."

Larson Medicine Horse, Age 50,
Chief Deputy Sheriff and Crow Sundance Chief,
Hardin, Montana

Two things hold me in awe: the starry heaven above me; and the moral law within me.

Immanuel Kant

"THE REAL question is this: How do we know what God is really like?

The answer is found in a very important principle: We only know what God is like because He has revealed or shown Himself to us. How did God show us what He is like? He has done it in various ways; we are not left to grope around in the dark and guess about God. For example, we see something of His power and wisdom by looking at the grandeur and order of nature. But supremely God has revealed Himself in a way which staggers our imagination: He took it upon Himself human flesh, and became a human being. Do you want to know—really know—what God is like? Then look at Jesus Christ, for 'He is the image of the invisible' (Colossians 1:15).

"Why did God do this? He did it because He loves us and wants us to know Him. Most of all, through Christ He removed the barrier of sin which separates us from God. This is why the most important thing we can do in our search for God is to look at Christ as He is found in the pages of the New Testament—and open our lives to Him."

Billy Graham, Age 71, Evangelist,
Charlotte, North Carolina

"THE FEELING I get from the word 'God' is one of love. I think He is a very different kind of being, a kind, gentle thing—in a way, Santa Claus comes to mind. I know Santa Claus is not real, but if he was, God would have the exact personality of him."

Lisa C. Hazen, Age 16,
Warwick, New York

To obey God is perfect liberty.

Seneca

"I THINK the power of life that runs through us and pushes us to be more and do more and to actualize what we sense deeply we're meant to be —that's God. I remember once studying world history and thinking of the image of light. I wondered—what is the flame that leaps up? What is that quality human beings have when the light comes leaping through them? I think it's happening today in Czechoslovakia, and other parts of the world. There's a longing for freedom, a leaping up of the human spirit toward self-direction. It's like infants being drawn to the voice of a loving parent or a flower turning its face to the sun. That energy is God."

Janice DeJardine Tobie,
Associate in Ministry and Counselor,
Seattle, Washington

I shall always maintain that whoso says in his heart, "There is no God," while he takes the name of God upon his lips, is either a liar or a madman.

Jean-Jacques Rousseau

"I WORK WITH many people who are dying from AIDS. I was with one man friend who died this weekend. As he was dying, all his friends were gathered and he was trying very hard to be with us. As he died, there was a tremendous presence in the room with us. There was a love. There was a light. Call it God, Goddess, higher power, the source within. It was there and I could feel it as he crossed over to the other side."

Janie Spahr, Age 47,
Executive Director, Ministry of Light,
San Rafael, California

If man were free, God would cease to exist.

Georges Clemenceau

"I KNOW little about His or Her form, but a great deal about God's ways. God reveals Himself or Herself through laws of physics, chemistry, and medicine. These are mysterious forces on which people can depend. As there are physical laws, there are moral laws too. God is revealed in this sphere as well. When one finds peace by making a commitment to the eternal values of peace, justice, and love, one understands a second dimension of God."

Heslip M. "Happy" Lee, Age 68,
American Baptist Minister and Member of
Fundamentalists Anonymous,
Cedartown, Georgia

"BEING BORN again, I feel that my life has more meaning. Most of the people I know that don't really know God personally are still searching. They are like twenty-five-year-olds searching for the same things they were when they were fifteen. I'm not searching for acceptance. I'm not searching for love. I'm not searching for what am I going to do with my life. My life will always have meaning. I don't always have to be wondering, 'What am I going to do with my life?' 'What if everything doesn't work out?' 'What am I going to be doing twenty years from now?' 'Am I going to be a failure?' I feel I have peace because no matter what happens, I've given my life to the Lord. I know God's love. It's really given me a focus and direction in my life."

Regina Francke, Age 25, Housewife,
Garfield, New Jersey

"WHEN I think of God, I look at living things. My idea of God has grown as I have grown and each experience brings new insight. Seeing the immensity and awe-inspiring power of nature itself always forces me to reconsider the origins and meaning of 'existence.' Thunder and lightning, wind, earthquakes, and turbulent waters instantly evoke a sense of unfathomable power. But sometimes the simplest 'little' things contain equal amounts of God. Babies' fingernails, bugs, Popsicle sticks, smiles, tears . . . it's all how you look at it. 'God' is a way of seeing. God is the way you live your life and the realization that you are living."

Keith Haring, Age 31, Artist,
New York City

God is voluptuous and delicious.

Meister Eckhart

"GOD IS like an abstract painting that people can interpret in different ways."

Shaun Lockhart, Age 13,
Anchorage, Alaska

In the beginning was the word and the word was hydrogen gas.

Harlow Shapley

"**A**LTHOUGH the peoples of the world have realized that there are many definitions of God (as this project implies), there is only one, and in spite of mankind's misunderstandings, He remains the I AM who has told us in His Word. No matter what we mean when we say God, it has no real value unless God says it too."

Judith M. Chapman-Ward,
Age 40, Accounting Clerk,
Chicago, Illinois

If there were no God it would be necessary to invent Him.

Voltaire

What do you mean when you say God? The following space is provided for you to record your own thoughts on this question.

Readers who wish to participate in the next book are invited to send responses of fifty words or less to the question What Do We Mean When We Say Love? to Love Book, Box 6V, 96 Henry Street, Brooklyn, New York 11201. Please include your full name, address, age, and occupation. All entries are the property of the authors and will not be returned.